Motorcycle-Mania!

By David Kimber and Richard Newland

Gareth Stevens Publishing
A WORLD ALMANAC EDUCATION GROUP COMPANY

Please visit our web site at: www.garethstevens.com
For a free color catalog describing Gareth Stevens Publishing's list
of high-quality books and multimedia programs, call 1-800-542-2595 (USA)
or 1-800-387-3178 (Canada). Gareth Stevens Publishing's fax: (414) 332-3567.

Library of Congress Cataloging-in-Publication Data

Kimber, David, 1960–
    Motorcycle-mania! / by David Kimber and Richard Newland. — North American ed.
      p. cm. — (Vehicle-mania!)
    Includes index.
    Contents: Aprilia RSV Mille R — Benelli Tornado — Buell XB9R Firebolt — Honda CBR1100XX Blackbird —
Kawasaki Ninja ZX-12R — Mondial Piega — Harley-Davidson V-Rod — Cagiva V-Raptor 1000 — Ducati 999R —
MV Agusta F4 SPR Senna — Suzuki GSX 1300R Hayabusa — Triumph Daytona 955i — Yamaha YZF R1.
    ISBN 0-8368-3783-5 (lib. bdg.)
    1. Motorcycles—Juvenile literature. [1. Motorcycles.] I. Newland, Richard. II. Title. III. Series.
TL440.15.K56   2003
629.227'5—dc21
                                                 2003043919

This North American edition first published in 2004 by
Gareth Stevens Publishing
A World Almanac Education Group Company
330 West Olive Street, Suite 100
Milwaukee, Wisconsin 53212

This U.S. edition copyright © 2004 by Gareth Stevens Inc. Original edition copyright © 2003 ticktock Entertainment Ltd.
First published in Great Britain in 2003 by ticktock Media Ltd., Unit 2, Orchard Business Centre, North Farm Road,
Tunbridge Wells, Kent, TN2 3XF, United Kingdom.

We would like to thank: Jamie Asher, Richard Newland of *Fast Bikes* magazine, and Elizabeth Wiggans.

Gareth Stevens Editor: Jim Mezzanotte
Gareth Stevens Art Direction: Tammy Gruenewald

All images Car Photo Library — www.carphoto.co.uk.

Printed in Hong Kong

1 2 3 4 5 6 7 8 9 07 06 05 04 03

CONTENTS

APRILIA RSV MILLE R 4

BENELLI TORNADO 6

BUELL XB9R FIREBOLT 8

HONDA CBR1100XX BLACKBIRD 10

KAWASAKI NINJA ZX-12R 12

MONDIAL PIEGA 14

HARLEY-DAVIDSON V-ROD 16

CAGIVA V-RAPTOR 1000 18

DUCATI 999R 20

MV AGUSTA F4 SPR SENNA 22

SUZUKI GSX 1300R HAYABUSA 24

TRIUMPH DAYTONA 955i 26

YAMAHA YZF R1 28

GLOSSARY 30

INDEX 32

APRILIA RSV MILLE R

Aprilia is an Italian company that first became known for making bicycles. In 1968, the company began building motorcycles and mopeds. Aprilia started selling the RSV Mille R in 2000. The engine has only two **cylinders,** but it produces a lot of **horsepower.** This beautiful machine is the fastest bike Aprilia has ever built.

Did You Know?

Mille **means "thousand" in Italian. The RSV Mille R gets its name from its engine size, which is almost 1,000 cubic centimeters (cc).**

Until the end of 2001, an RSV Mille R only came with one seat. Then, in 2002, Aprilia made a two-seater version.

Unlike most motorcycles, the RSV Mille R has three headlights.

FACTS AND STATS

First Model Year:
2000

Origin: Italy

Weight:
370 pounds (168 kilograms)

Fuel Tank Capacity:
4.8 gallons (18 liters)

Available Colors:
Yellow or Aprilia Black

Engine Size: 997.6 cc

Engine Cylinders: 2

Maximum Power:
128 horsepower (hp)

Number of Gears: 6

Maximum Speed:
168 miles (270 kilometers) per hour

The RSV Mille R has special **disc brakes** that are very powerful. A rider can stop the RSV Mille R in an amazingly short period of time.

BENELLI TORNADO

The Italian company Benelli was founded in 1911 by a widow named Teresa Benelli. She started the business to provide jobs for her six sons. At first, the company made spare parts for motorcyles and cars. Then, in 1921, Benelli built its first motorcycle. The company eventually became famous for making successful racing bikes. In 2002, Benelli began selling the extremely fast Tornado.

The Tornado's engine is actually part of the **frame**, so the bike is very strong.

Did You Know?

Although the Tornado is built in Italy, it was designed by an Englishman and uses **suspension** made in Sweden.

Two big fans suck in air to cool the **radiator**, which is located under the seat.

FACTS AND STATS

First Model Year:
2002

Origin:
Italy

Weight:
408 pounds (185 kg)

Fuel Tank Capacity:
4.8 gallons (18 l)

Available Colors:
Green/Silver

Engine Size: 898 cc

Engine Cylinders: 3

Maximum Power: 147 hp

Number of Gears: 6

Maximum Speed:
162 miles (260 km) per hour

A more powerful racing version of the Tornado has competed in the **World Superbike Championship.** It was designed by Riccardo Rosa, who has worked with the Italian car company Ferrari.

BUELL XB9R FIREBOLT

Erik Buell started the Buell Motor Company in 1993, with help from Harley-Davidson. Although Harley-Davidson motorcycles have powerful engines, the bikes can also be heavy. Buell had an idea — he would use a Harley-Davidson engine in a lighter bike to make a really fast machine.

Did You Know?

Weighing just 386 pounds (175 kg), the Firebolt is one of the lightest **sportbikes** in the world.

The Firebolt uses a belt instead of a chain to turn the back wheel.

The Firebolt has a perimeter brake on the front wheel. This brake helps stop the bike very quickly.

FACTS AND STATS

First Model Year:
2002

Origin:
United States

Weight:
386 pounds (175 kg)

Fuel Tank Capacity:
3.7 gallons (14 l)

Available Colors:
Arctic White, Battle Blue

Engine Size: 984 cc

Engine Cylinders: 2

Maximum Power: 92 hp

Number of Gears: 5

Maximum Speed:
130 miles (209 km)
per hour

Unlike most motorcycles, the Firebolt has an exhaust pipe located underneath the bike instead of to the side. The Firebolt also has a hollow frame that is used to hold fuel.

HONDA CBR1100XX BLACKBIRD

The Japanese company Honda is one of the largest motorcycle makers in the world. The Blackbird was the world's fastest street bike until another Japanese company, Suzuki, began selling the Hayabusa in 1998. The Blackbird is still incredibly fast. With a few changes to the engine, it can reach 200 miles (322 km) per hour.

Did You Know?

In 2001, a rider on a special Blackbird with a **turbocharger** did a wheelie at an amazing 201 miles (323 km) per hour!

The Blackbird has a system called linked brakes. With this system, pulling on either the front or back brake lever operates both brakes.

Although the CBR900RR Fireblade is smaller than the Blackbird, the bike's lighter weight helps it race very fast. The Fireblade can reach 100 miles (161 km) per hour in 6 seconds.

FACTS AND STATS

First Model Year:
1996

Origin:
Japan

Weight:
492 pounds (223 kg)

Fuel Tank Capacity:
6.3 gallons (24 l)

Available Colors:
Black, Blue, or Red

Engine Size: 1,137 cc

Engine Cylinders: 4

Maximum Power: 164 hp

Number of Gears: 6

Maximum Speed:
174 miles (280 km) per hour

The Blackbird has awesome **acceleration.** Thanks to a powerful **inline-4 engine** and a sleek shape, it can reach 130 miles (209 km) per hour in 11 seconds.

KAWASAKI NINJA ZX-12R

Kawasaki is a Japanese company that has always made very fast motorcycles. The company's Ninja ZX-12R is currently the fastest bike on the planet, with a top speed of almost 200 miles (322 km) per hour. The Ninja has a large fuel tank, so the bike can be ridden for long distances without stopping.

The ZX-12R can come to a complete stop from a speed of 70 miles (113 km) per hour in less than 4 seconds.

A scoop under the headlight forces air to the bike's engine. A large amount of air helps the engine produce its incredible power.

FACTS AND STATS

First Model Year:
2000

Origin:
Japan

Weight:
463 pounds (210 kg)

Fuel Tank Capacity:
5.3 gallons (20 l)

Available Colors:
Black/Gold, Silver,
or Kawasaki Green

Engine Size: 1,199 cc

Engine Cylinders: 4

Maximum Power: 165 hp

Number of Gears: 6

Maximum Speed:
190 miles (306 km) per hour

Kawasaki's aircraft division helped create the ZX-12R's **fairing**. Using **aerodynamics**, designers created a fairing that helps the ZX-12R to be fast and stable at high speeds.

MONDIAL PIEGA

Mondial was founded by an Italian named Earl Boselli. His bikes won many races, especially in the 1950s, but Mondial eventually went out of business. In 2000, a new company was formed with the Mondial name. The fast and beautiful Piega is the first new Mondial motorcycle to be sold in thirty years.

The engine in the Piega comes from the Japanese company Honda. Mondial has made some changes to the engine so it produces even more horsepower.

Did You Know?

The president of Mondial is an Italian businessman named Roberto Ziletti. He loves motorcycles, so he decided to create a new company to build them.

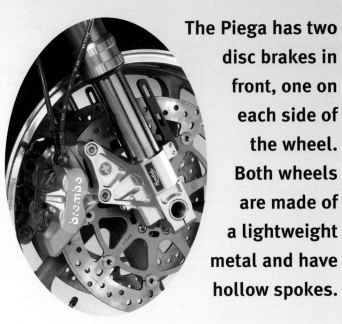

The Piega has two disc brakes in front, one on each side of the wheel. Both wheels are made of a lightweight metal and have hollow spokes.

FACTS AND STATS

First Model Year:
2002

Origin:
Italy

Weight:
498 pounds (226 kg)

Fuel Tank Capacity:
5.3 gallons (20 l)

Available Colors:
Silver/Blue or Black

Engine Size: 999 cc

Engine Cylinders: 2

Maximum Power: 140 hp

Number of Gears: 6

Maximum Speed:
161 miles (259 km) per hour

To keep down the weight of the Piega, Mondial used **carbon fiber** for the fairing and **aluminum** for the gas tank.

HARLEY-DAVIDSON V-ROD

Harley-Davidson is famous for making big, comfortable bikes that are fun to ride long distances on the open highway. The company's new V-Rod is similar to other models, but it is also different. Although this big bike is great for cruising, it is a brand new design with an extremely powerful engine. The sporty V-Rod is the fastest bike Harley-Davidson has ever made.

Did You Know?

Although Harley-Davidson motorcycles are heavy, the famous stunt rider Evel Knievel did all his jumps on a Harley-Davidson.

The V-Rod's fuel tank is actually located under the seat to make room for air **intakes** at the front of the bike. The intakes force air into the engine for greater power.

The **emblem** on the 2003 V-Rod has the number 100. This number refers to Harley-Davidson's hundredth anniversary in 2003.

FACTS AND STATS

First Model Year:
2002

Origin:
United States

Weight:
595 pounds (270 kg)

Fuel Tank Capacity:
4 gallons (15.1 l)

Available Colors:
Silver

Engine Size: 1,130 cc

Engine Cylinders: 2

Maximum Power: 115 hp

Number of Gears: 5

Maximum Speed:
135 miles (217 km) per hour

Harley-Davidson designed the new **liquid-cooled engine** with help from the German sports car maker Porsche.

CAGIVA V-RAPTOR 1000

Did You Know?

The name Cagiva is made up of the first two letters of the founder's last name (Castiglioni) and first name (Giovanni) and the first two letters of the town where the company is located (Varese).

The Italian company Cagiva built its first two motorcycles in 1978. A year later, the company was making over 40,000 bikes! The Raptor was designed by Miguel Galluzzi. It resembles another bike he designed — the famous Monster, built by the Italian company Ducati.

The "V" in the name V-Raptor refers to the bike's large and powerful V2 engine. This engine is made by the Japanese company Suzuki.

The V-Raptor actually has a set of "claws" by the passenger footrest!

The V-Raptor is called a "naked" bike because it does not have a fairing to cover the engine and other parts.

DUCATI 999R

The 999R is the fastest and most expensive model sold by the Italian company Ducati. It has a very powerful engine, and it is made of lightweight carbon and aluminum. The 999R can be driven on the street, but this powerful bike can also be used for racing.

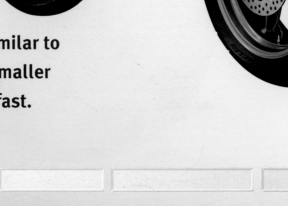

The Ducati 749 is very similar to the 999R, but it has a smaller engine and is not as fast.

People of all sizes can ride comfortably on the 999R. The bike's seat and fuel tank can be moved backward and forward, and its footrests can be moved up and down.

FACTS AND STATS

First Model Year:
2002

Origin:
Italy

Weight:
426 pounds (193 kg)

Fuel Tank Capacity:
4 gallons (15.5 l)

Available Colors:
Red

Engine Size: 999 cc

Engine Cylinders: 2

Maximum Power: 139 hp

Number of Gears: 6

Maximum Speed:
175 miles (282 km) per hour

Only 800 999R models have been built. Each 999R has a special silver plate that identifies it.

MV AGUSTA F4 SPR SENNA

MV Agusta is another Italian company with a long and successful racing history. Agusta bikes won 270 races between 1950 and 1975. The company went out of business, but in 1999 a new bike was built with the Agusta name — the stunning F4. The F4 SPR Senna is a special F4 named after Ayrton Senna, a race car driver from Brazil who died in a racing accident in 1994.

The Senna's exhaust pipes are located under the seat instead of on the side of the bike.

Did You Know?

Whenever a Senna is sold, some of the money is given to the Senna Foundation, which helps poor children in Brazil.

The Senna's sleek fairing has two headlights. One headlight is stacked on top of the other.

FACTS AND STATS

First Model Year:
2002

Origin:
Italy

Weight:
415 pounds (188 kg)

Fuel Tank Capacity:
5.3 gallons (20 l)

Available Colors:
Gray or Red

Engine Size: 749 cc

Engine Cylinders: 4

Maximum Power: 140 hp

Number of Gears: 6

Maximum Speed:
177 miles (285 km) per hour

Ayrton Senna and the president of MV Agusta were friends. The company built only 300 Sennas, which were created to honor the famous driver.

SUZUKI GSX 1300R HAYABUSA

The Japanese company Suzuki was formed in 1952. Since then, the company has built many kinds of motorcycles. Suzuki began selling the Hayabusa in 1998. At the time, it was the fastest bike in the world. The Hayabusa's engine is larger than some car engines.

Did You Know?

The Hayabusa is so powerful that it can wear out its back tire after just a thousand miles.

The GSX-R1000 is similar to the Hayabusa, but it is smaller and lighter.

The British Land Speed Record for a motorcycle is held by a turbocharged Hayabusa. The bike reached a speed of over 241 miles (388 km) per hour.

FACTS AND STATS

First Model Year:
1998

Origin:
Japan

Weight:
474 pounds (215 kg)

Fuel Tank Capacity:
4.8 gallons (18 l)

Available Colors:
Blue/Black, Blue/Silver, or Silver

Engine Size: 1,298 cc

Engine Cylinders: 4

Maximum Power: 155 hp

Number of Gears: 6

Maximum Speed:
186 miles (300 km) per hour

The hayabusa is a bird in Japan that eats blackbirds. Suzuki named its new sportbike after this bird because the bike is faster and more powerful than the Honda Blackbird.

TRIUMPH DAYTONA 955i

The British company Triumph was founded in 1902 and is one of the oldest motorcycle makers in the world. Triumph began selling the Daytona 955i in 1997, and since then it has improved the bike many times. The Daytona is the only British sportbike that can keep up with the fastest motorcycles from Japan and Italy.

Triumph first made the Speed-Twin (left) in 1937. The company's popular Bonneville, which it first sold in 1959, was based on the Speed-Twin.

The Daytona has an aluminum frame and a powerful three-cylinder engine. It is an extremely fast bike.

Triumph also makes a bike called the Speed Triple. This bike is very similar to the Daytona but does not have a fairing.

FACTS AND STATS

First Model Year:
1997

Origin:
Britain

Weight:
421 pounds (191 kg)

Fuel Tank Capacity:
5.5 gallons (21 l)

Available Colors:
Jet Black, Acidic Yellow, or Tornado Red

Engine Size: 955 cc

Engine Cylinders: 3

Maximum Power: 147 hp

Number of Gears: 6

Maximum Speed:
165 miles (265 km) per hour

Did You Know?

A Daytona was featured in the movie *Mission Impossible 2*, starring Tom Cruise.

YAMAHA YZF R1

Yamaha is one of the world's best known motorcycle makers. At first, this Japanese company only produced musical instruments, but after World War II it also began making motorcycles. Yamaha first sold the YZF R1 in 1997, and it was a huge success. In 2002, Yamaha began selling a new R1. The R1 is now better than ever!

Did You Know?

The R1 will reach a speed of 75 miles (121 km) per hour in first gear and over 100 miles (161 km) per hour in second gear.

The R1 does not use a light bulb for its rear light. Instead, it has many small **light-emitting diodes**, or LEDs. If one LED stops working, the other LEDs still provide light.

The YZF-R6 is one of Yamaha's most popular bikes. This small and light bike is not as fast as the R1, but it is excellent for twisting roads.

FACTS AND STATS

First Model Year:
2002

Origin:
Japan

Weight:
384 pounds (174 kg)

Fuel Tank Capacity:
4.8 gallons (18 l)

Available Colors:
Blue, Red, or White

Engine Size: 998 cc

Engine Cylinders: 4

Maximum Power: 152 hp

Number of Gears: 6

Maximum Speed:
176 miles (283 km) per hour

The new R1 is lighter than the original R1, and it also has a more powerful engine. The fairing on the new bike has a better aerodynamic shape.

GLOSSARY

acceleration: an increase in the speed of a vehicle.

aerodynamics: the study of how vehicles cut through the air.

aluminum: a lightweight metal that is often used in the construction of motorcycles and other vehicles.

carbon fiber: a threadlike material that is light and very strong.

cylinders: can-shaped spaces in an engine where a mixture of fuel and air explodes to create the engine's power.

disc brakes: a brake system that uses metal discs attached to the wheels and devices called calipers that squeeze the discs.

emblem: on a motorcycle, a figure or design that identifies the motorcycle maker.

fairing: the outer covering of a motorcycle that protects the rider and helps the bike cut through the air.

frame: the structure that supports the different parts of a motorcycle.

horsepower: a unit of measurement for an engine's power that was originally based on the pulling strength of a horse.

inline-4 engine: an engine with four cylinders arranged vertically in a row.

intakes: openings that can let in air or liquid.

light-emitting diodes (LEDs): small chips that give off light when electricity is applied to them and use less power than lightbulbs.

liquid-cooled engine: an engine that stays cool by pumping a liquid around the cylinders and through the radiator.

perimeter brake: a kind of disc brake that uses a disc attached to the outer rim of the wheel.

radiator: a piece of equipment that keeps an engine from getting too hot by cooling the liquid that flows around the cylinders.

sportbikes: high-performance street bikes, often based on racing bikes, that are not usually practical for long trips and often have room for just one person.

suspension: the parts of a motorcycle that attach the wheels to the frame and keep the motorcycle steady over bumps in the road.

turbocharger: a device that forces extra air into an engine's cylinders to increase horsepower.

World Superbike Championship: a racing series that features extremely fast bikes on paved racetracks with many twists and turns.

V2 engine: an engine that has two cylinders arranged in a "V" shape.

INDEX

A

acceleration 11, 24
aerodynamics 13, 29
aluminum 15, 20, 26
Aprilia 4
Aprilia RSV Mille R
  4, 5

B

belts 8
Benelli 6
Benelli, Teresa 6
Benelli Tornado 6, 7
Boselli, Earl 14
brakes 5, 9, 10, 15
Brazil 22
Britain 26, 27
British Land Speed
  Record 25
Buell 8
Buell, Erik 8
Buell XB9R
  Firebolt 8, 9

C

Cagiva 18
Cagiva V-Raptor 1000
  18, 19
carbon fiber 15, 20
Castiglioni,
  Giovanni 18

D

Ducati 18, 20
Ducati 749 20
Ducati 999R 20, 21

E

emblems 17
exhaust pipes 9, 22

F

fairings 13, 15,
  19, 27
Ferrari 7
footrests 19, 21
frames 6, 9
fuel tanks 12, 16, 21

G

Galluzzi, Miguel 18
Germany 17

H

Harley-Davidson 8,
  16, 17
Harley-Davidson
  V-Rod 16, 17
headlights 5, 12, 23
Honda 10, 14, 25
Honda CBR900RR
  Fireblade 11
Honda CBR1100XX
  Blackbird 10,
  11, 25

I

inline-4 engine 11
Italy 4, 5, 6, 7, 14,
  15, 18, 19, 20, 21,
  22, 23, 26

J

Japan 10, 11, 12, 13,
  14, 18, 24, 25, 26,
  28, 29

K

Kawasaki 12, 13
Kawasaki Ninja
  ZX-12R 12, 13

Knievel, Evel 16

L

light-emitting diodes
  (LEDs) 28
linked brakes 10

M

*Mission
  Impossible 2* 27
Mondial 14, 15
Mondial
  Piega 14, 15
mopeds 4
MV Agusta 22, 23
MV Agusta F4 SPR
  Senna 22, 23

P

perimeter brakes 9
Porsche 17

R

radiators 7
rear lights 28

S

seats 4, 7, 16, 21, 22
Senna,
  Ayrton 22, 23
suspension 6
Suzuki 10, 18, 24, 25
Suzuki GSX 1300R
  Hayabusa 10,
  24, 25
Suzuki
  GSX-R1000 24
Sweden 6

T

Triumph 26, 27

Triumph
  Bonneville 26
Triumph Daytona
  955i 26, 27
Triumph
  Speed Triple 27
Triumph
  Speed-Twin 26
turbochargers 10, 25
tires 13, 24

U

United States 9, 17

V

V2 engine 18

W

wheelies 10
wheels 8, 9, 15
World Superbike
  Championship
  7, 20

Y

Yamaha 28, 29
Yamaha
  YZF R1 28, 29
Yamaha YZF-R6 29

Z

Ziletti, Roberto 14